I0421471

How to Write

A Nonfiction

Book That Sells

By Christine John

http://www.ChristineJohnBooks.com

How to Write a Nonfiction Book That Sells

Copyright © 2015 by Christine John

Email: christinejohnbooks@gmail.com

Website: www.ChristineJohnBooks.com

Front Cover Image: Courtesy of Sixninepixels at FreeDigitalPhotos.net

Disclaimer:

Although the author has made every effort to ensure that the information in this book was correct at press time, the author does not assume and hereby disclaim any liability to any party for any loss, damage, or disruption caused by errors or omissions, whether such errors or omissions result from negligence, accident, or any other cause.

Contents

Get Ready to Write!

Do you need help writing your first nonfiction book? Do you have a great idea for a book but don't know how to get started writing it? Are you worried that it might take too long and that you don't have enough time to write? Then you have made the right decision in purchasing this nonfiction writing guide.

If you are a new author or an established writer, ***How to Write a Nonfiction Book that Sells*** will show you step by step how to research and write a nonfiction book that people will want to read. You will learn how to research your idea for your book to ensure that it is a topic that people are searching for. Discover two different methods of creating an outline for your book. Additionally, this book will show you the best way to edit your book and how to design an attention-grabbing book cover.

From a very early age, I had always dreamed of becoming an author. I enjoy writing books and it wasn't until 2012 when I finally got the opportunity to self-publish my very first book ***How to Start and Run an Online Business***.

Three years and eight books later, I chose to write this book for first time writers who have dreamed of publishing a nonfiction book, but have no idea how to get started. I hope that this book will help and inspire you to begin working on your nonfiction book.

This guide is divided into eight chapters. Each chapter walks you through each stage of the process of writing your book from finding the perfect place to write to researching the topic you want to write about. From getting down to actually writing your book to editing it and designing the perfect book cover.

Writing a nonfiction book can be a rewarding experience, especially when you believe that the book you are writing will help millions of people all over the world. This guide will take all the frustration out of writing your first nonfiction book. Once you finish reading ***How to Write a Nonfiction Book that Sells***, you would have come up with a brilliant topic to write about and you would be following the steps laid out in this guide to write your first nonfiction book. So let's move on to the first chapter and get started now!

Chapter 1: Seven Tips to Become a Highly Effective Nonfiction Author

In order to become a highly effective nonfiction author, you have to be efficient. This doesn't mean that you have to spend all your time writing. It simply means that you need to know what the best time to write is and how you will get it done in the time you want to have it completed. So let's look at seven ways you can become a highly effective nonfiction author.

1. Make Time for Your Writing

You need to set aside a specific time for your writing. Develop a routine. At what time of the day do you feel the most productive? Some writers feel the most creative in the mornings, whereas others prefer to work in the evenings. Come up with a time in which you can dedicate to your writing without any distractions.

2. Create an Outline

You should always start with an outline, whether you are writing an article or a book. Creating an outline first makes the whole process of writing a lot easier and you will notice that you finish your work a lot faster as well. An outline helps you to stay focussed on the topic you are writing about and it helps your work to flow smoothly.

3. Write Your First Draft

After you have created your outline, start writing your first draft. Let your creative juices flow. Forget about trying to edit your work because this will only slow down your writing and it will cause you to lose momentum. Don't worry about spelling or grammatical mistakes. Don't worry about whether it makes sense or not. You will have plenty of time to edit your work later. Just keep writing and get all of your ideas down on paper before you forget what you had planned to write.

4. Rewrite Your First Draft

Once you have completed your first draft put it aside for 24 hours. Give yourself a break and come back to it later. Then start to rewrite your first draft. You will notice that when you rewrite your book it will improve your writing and the book will come out better.

5. Ignore that Negative Voice in Your Head

While you are writing you may start to doubt yourself. You may get that negative feeling that what you're writing is not good enough and that you might as well give up. Ignore that negative voice and just keep on writing. Follow the outline you created, develop a daily routine of writing and you will finish your book.

6. Have Confidence in Yourself

Writing your first nonfiction book may seem like a daunting task, but you can do it. You may not feel very confident at first, but if you keep on writing you will get better and your confidence will improve.

7. Don't Stop Reading

If you want to become a highly effective writer, then you need to do a lot of reading. Many writers get inspired by the books they read. They examine the writing styles of other authors and they use what moves them to improve their writing. Reading also helps you to improve your vocabulary.

So in order to become a highly effective nonfiction author you need to sit down and write. It is easy to get distracted, to make excuses, and to procrastinate. But if you have a message that you want to share with the world then you need to get rid of any obstacles in your way and sit down and start writing.

Chapter 2: How to Find the Perfect Writing Environment

If you are planning to have a writing career then you will need a place where you can work undisturbed. This place has to be in an area where there are little distractions. It should also be in an area where you feel comfortable and where you can be creative and feel inspired. So how do you find a place where you can concentrate on your writing? Well, the best way to find the perfect writing environment is to create one. The following five steps will help you to find your perfect writing space.

1. Find a place where you love to work. It could be anywhere you feel inspired and like to work, for example, your bedroom, living room or home office.

2. Remove everything that may distract or annoy you. Different types of noises can distract you from your writing, such as noise from next door neighbours, children playing, as well as emails and social media. Turn off your mobile phone and the television set. Remove all the clutter from your

work environment like loads of laundry or a messy desk.

3. Do you find it difficult to work at home? Then change your work space. You can do your writing at the local library or find a quiet area in the park where you can work.

4. Find someplace that isn't too noisy where you can write. Not everyone can concentrate on writing when their environment is too quiet. Some like to hear sounds of nature, background music or the distant noise of traffic to help them focus on their writing. On the other hand, other people need a completely quiet environment to focus on their work. Make sure that the area where you work is free from noise and distractions.

5. Make your work environment beautiful. Decorate it with photos of your favourite destinations, buy fresh flowers or some nice scented candles. Buy a comfortable chair, a pillow to support your back, or a table designed specifically to hold your laptop. Do whatever is necessary to make your workspace more comfortable and enjoyable so that you will spend more time writing.

Chapter 3: Seven Steps to Getting Outstanding Nonfiction Ideas

The hardest part about being a writer is coming up with great ideas for a new book. It can be even more challenging if you are a first time author.

As a writer you cannot just sit back and wait for inspiration to strike. If you plan on building a successful writing business then you need to come up with profitable ideas every single day. There is a method that you can use to ensure that you always get ideas simply by following the seven steps listed below:

Step 1: Collect Your Information

Information can be found all around you. The information you gather is where all of your ideas will come from. You can collect general information, which is just about anything you find interesting, or you can gather specific information which is related to a topic you have chosen to write about. The material you gather can come from your general knowledge and education, reading books, watching television, or surfing the internet. Now that you have gathered all the data you need, it is time to move on to the next step which is examining the information.

Step 2: Examine the Information

Go through all the raw data you have collected and put together what you feel makes sense and remove the information that seems irrelevant. Look at the material from different angles and see how they all fit together. Any ideas you come up with at this stage, write them all down. Don't stop to think about what order they should be in or how your ideas will flow. All that will come later.

Step 3: Let the Information Simmer

At this stage you need to take all the hard work you did in gathering and sifting through the information, put it aside for a while and take a break. Let all that raw data you put together simmer in your mind. Take a time out and do something else. Take a walk in the park, try reading, or listening to music. You can even take a nice warm bath and let that spark of inspiration strike!

Step 4: Let Your Ideas Flow

You should be bursting with ideas at this stage. The answers you were looking for may seem to leap into your mind out of nowhere.

Some ideas may seem fantastic and others may not be that great. Whatever ideas you come up with, write them all down. If, however, at this stage you still have not come up with any brilliant ideas, don't give up. Keep on writing and jot down any thoughts that may enter your mind. Then move on to the next step.

Step 5: Start to Develop Your Idea

This is where you start to use your writing skills. Whatever the idea you came up with, mould it and shape it until it becomes something real that you can write about. Try creating a mind map to organize your ideas. Start with your main idea and write down all other ideas associated with your main (central) idea.

Step 6: Tell Others About Your Idea

Share your idea with others. Talk to people who you can trust to help you to improve your idea. They may add to it or make some changes to it. Sharing your idea with others may also help you to be more creative and come up with even better ideas.

Step 7: Repeat the Whole Process

Remember in Step 6 you were advised to share your ideas. The feedback you get from the previous step should be used to add to the data you gathered in Step 1. Then move on two Step 2, sifting through the new data with the existing information you gathered. Then repeat Steps 3, 4, 5 and 6. Keep this going until you have thought up the best idea for your book.

The easiest part is coming up with ideas. The most difficult part is taking those ideas and writing a book that your target audience will want to buy. But don't be discouraged if it takes you a bit longer to come up with ideas. The next chapter gives a more detailed description as to what you need to do to come up with ideas. This should help you to gather the information you need to write an outstanding nonfiction book that people will want to read.

Chapter 4: Research Your Topic

Welcome to the first step to getting your book published. Before you decide on what you are going to write about you need to research your topic to ensure that it is a popular subject that people are searching for and that it will be profitable. The main objective of writing a nonfiction book is to generate sales. Therefore the key to writing nonfiction is to connect with a particular audience by offering them what they are looking for.

As part of your research the first thing you need to do is to come up with some ideas for a book. What are you interested in? It is always better to think of something that interests you and then find out if other people share the same interest. This will make writing a book that much easier and more enjoyable. So take out a pen and paper and start writing down some ideas and then find out whether there is a potential audience who would also be interested in reading your book.

Come Up with Ideas

There are many areas of your life that could inspire you to write a book. You could start by thinking about your job, your hobbies, and things that you have experienced throughout your life.

For example, consider the type of job that you do. You don't necessarily have to be an employee. You could also be a student, a homemaker, or a volunteer worker. Maybe you have a specialized skill that would be of interest to other people. The fact that you are doing a particular type of job, it means that you already know more than the majority of the population about this subject.

If, however, you don't find that your work experience is very exciting or is not interesting enough to write about then you can think about other jobs you did in the past or your hobbies and leisure interests. Do you like to play football or basketball? Are you good at playing piano or guitar? Do you enjoy cake decorating? Do you know how to make paper airplanes? Whatever your interests are, there are bound to be thousands of other people around the globe who share the same interests.

If you do decide to write a book about your hobby, find out if there are other people who share the same interest. Do a search online for clubs or organizations that are dedicated to this hobby. Are there magazines that focus on your particular topic?

For example, there are magazines which focus on the topic of photography, nature, knitting, etc. If you do find magazines on your chosen topic find out what is their circulation. It is highly recommended that you look for a potential audience of at least 200,000 to make your book writing efforts worthwhile.

Additionally, think about any life experiences you may have had. You may have planned a wedding, had a baby, had a death in the family, bought your first home, or started your own business. There is a wide range of topics that you can write about that other people may be searching for.

There are a wide range of topics that you can write about and it would be beneficial to you if you search for other books on your topic in library catalogues, in major bookstores, or on Amazon. If you find hundreds of recent titles, then the market may be saturated meaning that if you were to write on the same topic you may not get a lot of sales. On the other hand, if there are hardly any other books, that could mean there isn't much interest in that topic.

If you want to write a nonfiction book that will one day become a best seller, you may need to focus on a topic that addresses a universal theme that could consistently generate a lot of sales. The following topics should give you some idea as to the type of information that people tend to search for daily online. If you do a search on Amazon, you will notice that many of the bestselling nonfiction books focus on these major topics as well:

Making Money

Make money from home

Make money with your camera

Make money selling stuff on eBay

Make money without a job

Make money with a blog

Make money on the internet

Make money in property

Saving Money

Save money on food

Save money for kids

Save money on car insurance

Save money on petrol

Save money on heating

Save money for a house

Save money for traveling

Save money on airline tickets

Investing Money

Investing in oil

Investing in shares

Investing in gold

Investing in the stock market

Investing in mutual funds

Investing in bonds

Personal Improvement

Improve your self esteem

Improve your memory

Improve your posture

Increase self confidence

Increase your vocabulary

How-to Information

How to get married

How to get rid of a cold

How to deal with bereavement

How to cope with divorce

How to buy/sell a house

How to buy a car

How to make your own clothes

How to design a garden

How to get a job

How to start your own business

Health and Fitness

Lowering your blood pressure

How to reduce stress

Detoxify your body

Fitness plan for men

Fitness plan for women

Anti-aging remedies

How to change your eating habits

How to reduce back pain

Cure tooth decay

Teach your child to sleep

Diet and Weight Loss

Walking for weight loss

Smoothies for weight loss

Jump rope workouts

Clean food diet (avoiding processed foods)

Healthy eating for diabetics

Healthy eating for vegetarians

How to lose belly fat

Low carb diet

Dating and Personal Relationships

How to find love

How to break up with your boyfriend/girlfriend

How to get your ex back

How to attract men

How to attract women

Dating do's and don'ts

Dating advice for women

Dating advice for men

How to make every man want you

The three biggest desires most people have are wealth, health and happiness. Therefore, people will be willing to pay for information that helps them to achieve these three desires quickly and easily.

As I mentioned above, the other highly profitable category for writing nonfiction books is how-to information. People want solutions to their problems and they want to achieve their dreams.

So if you can show them how to make more money, how to lose weight, how to find love, or how to solve any common problem from building a bird feeder to the law of attraction – and how to do it easily and quickly – you can definitely sell a lot of books.

Once you have a general topic in mind, your next step is to figure out the specific way you can help your readers. Whatever subject you're writing about, you need to find out what problem your readers most need help with, what information they are desperately searching for, and what benefit they want most of all.

You may be able to discover what your potential readers want by talking to some of them. Join their forums. For example, you can do a Google search for parenting forums which give tips and advice to first time parents, or business forums that share advice and experiences for small businesses.

Visit Yahoo Answers and look up any questions people ask concerning your chosen topic. You can also join groups on Facebook and Twitter where you can find out how much interest there is in the topic you have chosen to write about.

To really have a career writing nonfiction, you need to provide tangible benefits to your readers. Bestselling nonfiction books are generally focused on one big idea that can be summarized in a few words (such as the title), strikes the reader as original, and is easy to understand and remember.

Just remember that what most readers want are easy answers and step-by-step solutions to their problems. If you want to target a large audience, keep your message simple and practical.

Keyword Research

If you want to sell your e-book then you need to make sure that it's a topic that other people are interested in. They should be so desperate for information that they will gladly pay to get the information conveniently delivered to them in the form of a book. One of the best ways to find out if you have chosen a profitable category to write about is to do keyword research.

What is Keyword Research?

Doing keyword research means that you are researching the actual search terms people enter into the search engines when conducting a search online. This usually involves finding the search volume and relative competitiveness of the terms. The outcome you should get from keyword research is to find out which set of keywords has a high number of searches per month which will in turn help you to decide what topics you should cover in your book.

Advantages of Doing Keyword Research

Keyword research may be one of the most important tools you will use when trying to decide on the best topics to write about. One of the advantages of doing keyword research is that when it is done correctly, keywords can literally unlock the door to a world of online customers searching for your book. The other advantage is that the internet makes it very easy to research the subjects people want to know about. You can learn a lot by analysing the queries people enter into search engines. One of the ways you can do this is by using a free online tool called Google Keyword Planner.

Google Keyword Planner

The Google Keyword Planner is a free AdWords tool that helps you to search for keyword and ad group ideas. You can also use it to get historical statistics and see how a list of keywords might perform. If you were using pay-per-click (PPC) advertising, then the AdWords tool can help you to choose competitive bids and budgets for your chosen keywords to use with your ad campaigns. However, we will only be focusing on keyword research and analysis so that you can have an idea of what topics you should write about in your book.

Keyword Planner is free to use but you must have a Google email address in order to use this tool. Once you have created your account go to the following website:

https://adwords.google.com/KeywordPlanner

1. Click **Sign In** and enter your email address and password.

2. To the right, click on the option ***Search for new keyword and ad group ideas***.

3. Enter a search term, for example, 'losing weight'.

4. Scroll down the page and click the blue button ***Get Ideas***.

5. You will see a list of ad group ideas but what you really want to look for are keyword ideas. So click on the **Keyword Ideas** tab.

The following results are part of the results list that appeared for the search term 'losing weight':

Keyword	Avg. Monthly Searches	Competition
Losing weight	12,100	Medium
How to lose weight quickly	18,100	Medium
Losing weight fast	2,900	Medium
Losing weight quickly	1,000	Medium
Quickest way to lose weight	5,400	Low
Lose weight quickly	1,900	Medium

You can see from the list above that the term 'losing weight' is a very popular topic about which there is a lot of interest. Any keyword or phrase with a monthly volume of 500 or more is definitely worth focusing on.

Additionally, it's very likely that a lot of people using these search terms will be seeking help urgently. Therefore, from the search results above you could definitely write a book on 'how to lose weight quickly' because this search term had the highest volume of monthly searches which was 18,100.

How to Use Your Keyword Research

Based on your keyword research, you should now have an idea as to the kind of information that people are searching for online in the category you have in mind, and you will also have some data on the search terms they are using. This is a great way to get started on deciding on a topic for your book.

The next step is to do a little more research on your chosen topic. You can perform a search on Clickbank, Google, Amazon, Facebook and Twitter.

Search on Clickbank

Clickbank is one of the largest online retailers on the web. This website features mainly informational digital products which can be downloaded instantly to customers in electronic format. Many of the world's top-selling e-books are listed on this site.

Go to http://www.clickbank.com and click on Marketplace on the top right.

Using the same example, enter your chosen term (losing weight) in the search box and click Enter.

Under 'Sort results by' click on the arrow and select 'Popularity'. This option allows the list items to be arranged in order of popularity.

The top five results which appeared in the list are:

1. The Venus Factor
2. The 3 Week Diet
3. Trouble Spot Nutrition
4. Fat Burning Kitchen
5. Body Weight Burn Fat Loss

Under each of these results you will notice some interesting figures given for each product as well. These are marketplace statistics which are very useful in determining the potential of various niches. These marketplace stats are defined as follows:

Initial $/sale: This is the average amount that an affiliate earns for each sale of this product.

Avg $/sale: For one-time purchases, this number is the same as Initial $/sale. For every new purchase of this product, this amount is the average you'd make in total over the life of a new customer.

Avg %/sale: This number shows the average commission rate earned for all sales of a vendor's products, including one-time purchases, rebills, and upsell purchases.

Grav: Short for Gravity, this number represents the number of different affiliates who successfully earned a commission by promoting this product. This number can give you an idea of what products are popular at the moment.

These statistics are mainly for affiliates who are interested in promoting products, but they are also very useful for researching the popularity of different niches. For example, if a product has a high gravity, this means that a lot of affiliates are promoting it successfully. This may mean that it may be a good niche to get into.

Do a Google Search

Further to your research you need to do a Google search to see if there are any other products on the market for your chosen keywords. Enter your search term in Google and see what results show up. On the results page you can see sponsored listings, which are paid advertisements, at the top and on the right side of the results page.

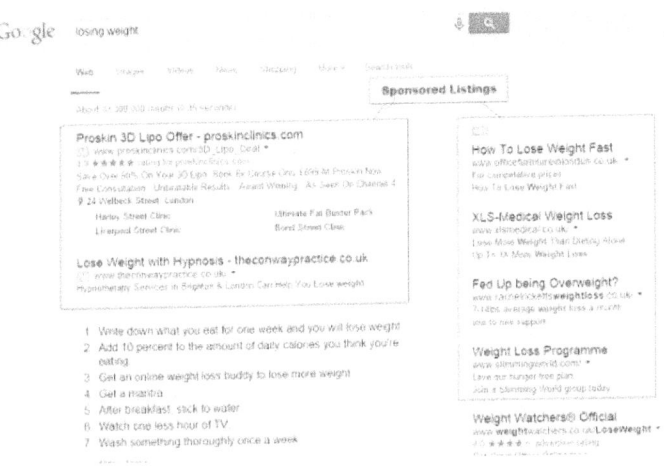

The sponsored results are especially important because this is where people pay to have their items listed. So we can assume that they are making money from their paid listings. If the results include e-books, check out their sales pages to see what features and benefits they offer to their prospective customers. Just like when you searched the Clickbank marketplace, consider how you could make your title different from the competition and make it more appealing to potential customers.

Search on Amazon

Amazon is another great place where you can perform your search as well. Amazon is one of the largest online bookstores on the web and it is here where you can find out the number of printed books, and e-books as well, that your title will be competing with. You can also get ideas looking at other book titles so that you can come up with a compelling title for your book.

Search on Facebook

You can also find out if there is a high volume of interest in your chosen topic by conducting a search on Facebook. Log in to your Facebook account. If you don't have one then you will need to sign up to create an account. In the search bar type in your chosen keyword and add the word 'posts' to it without the quotes. From the example above, we will use the term 'losing weight posts'.

In the results you will find a number of posts that were shared or posted on Facebook recently. Some of these posts are promoting e-books about losing weight. Under each of these posts you will find the number of people who liked, shared and commented on these posts. This data will help you to determine if the term 'losing weight' is a popular topic that a lot of people are talking about. This is also a great way to get ideas on topics you can cover in your book and to check out the different types of e-books that have been written about the subject.

Search on Twitter

Just like Facebook you can do keyword research on Twitter. Log in to your account and type 'losing weight' in the search bar. If you do not have an account with Twitter then you will need to create one before you can do your keyword research.

You can also use the hashtag and your chosen keyword to perform your search on Twitter. Simply type in the term '#losingweight' without the quotes and you will find results for people who have used this term in their Tweets. You will find on the results page a lot of photos, videos and links to articles about losing weight. You can see how popular this topic is and it also gives you ideas on what to include in your book.

Chapter 5: Create an Outline of Your Book

By this time you should have decided on the topic you're going to write about and performed your research to ensure that it is a popular topic that people are interested and willing to pay for. The next thing you are going to do is create an outline of your nonfiction book. As a nonfiction writer I highly recommend that you prepare an outline before you start the actual writing of your book. Doing an outline will make your writing a whole lot easier and faster to complete.

Why You Should Outline Your Book

There are five good reasons why you should outline your book first before writing it.

1. Creating an outline will greatly help you to organize your thoughts and structure your book.
2. Your ideas will flow naturally with a solid structure and foundation. And your writing will seem effortless.

3. An outline also helps you to divide your book into workable chunks so that you don't feel overwhelmed.

4. If you create an outline first, you can be sure that you will cover all the topics which need to be included in your book.

5. Additionally, by spending time creating an outline, you can ensure that all the topics are covered in the best order.

Different Methods of Outlining

There are two different methods that you can use to outline your book. You can use one or a combination of these methods. But make sure that you choose the method that you feel most comfortable with.

Outlining Method #1: Mind Mapping

Creating a mind map is one of the methods you can use to outline your nonfiction book. A mind map is a diagram which consists of one central idea surrounded by connected branches of subtopics that are associated with the central idea.

Creating a mind map is a very easy method that you can use to outline your book. First, get a blank sheet of paper and write your book's topic (or title) in the centre of the page. Next, write down all the ideas that you have around the edge. Draw circles around each idea and draw a line to connect your associated ideas to the central (main) idea. When you are sure that you have included all of your key ideas, the next thing you need to do is type all of this information onto your computer and organize them into chapters.

The following image is an example of a mind map created around the chosen topic 'losing weight'.

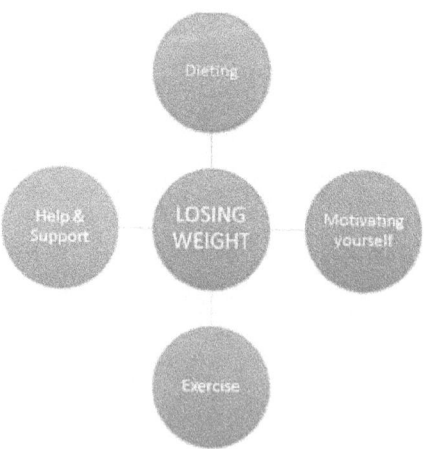

Outlining Method #2: Chapter by Chapter Outline

Not everyone likes the mind map method of creating an outline. Some writers prefer to outline their book chapter by chapter. I also prefer this outlining method because I feel that it is easier and faster to organize my key ideas into chapters. It also makes it easier for me to see if I have left out any useful subtopics that I may need to include in my book.

Although a chapter-by-chapter outline helps you to organize your thoughts and create a structure for your book, it can also be used as the basic table of contents. Your outline usually starts with the introduction and ends with the conclusion. In between are the chapters.

List all of the topics you want to cover in your book in the form of chapters and rearrange them until they are in the order you think is best. The best thing to do is to list the basic content at the beginning of your book and work up gradually to more advanced topics. We will now go into more detail as to how you should start the process of creating an outline for your book.

Step 1: Decide How Many Chapters Your Book will Contain

The first step to creating your outline is deciding on the number of chapters to include in your book. If you are not too sure about the material you want to include in each chapter then take a look at the table of contents in other books that are similar to your chosen topic. This will give you an idea of the number of chapters your book should have and what each chapter should cover.

Step 2: Decide What Information Will be Included in Each Chapter

Once you have chosen the number of chapters your book will contain, the next step is to decide what content will be included in each chapter. If you used the mind map outline, refer to the associated topics that you connected to your central idea.

The following example is a list of chapters that you may include in your book:

Introduction
The Problem with Dieting

How Weight Loss Works

Different Approaches to Losing Weight

How to Motivate Yourself to Lose Weight

Change the Way You Eat

Get Plenty of Exercise

Take care of your Body

Change Your Attitude Toward Your Health

Where to Get Help and Support

Conclusion

Create an Outline of Each Chapter

Once you have a list of all the chapters you want to include in your book, the next thing you need to do is create an outline of each chapter. In other words, make a list of all the topics you want to cover in each chapter.

Take one of the chapters you listed and think of all the topics you want to cover in that particular chapter and write them down in any order.

For example, for one of the chapters listed above, 'How to Motivate Yourself to Lose Weight', here are the following topics that need to be covered in that chapter:

How to Motivate Yourself to Lose Weight
1. Create a diet plan that fits with your lifestyle
2. Choose a realistic goal
3. Set your priorities for losing weight
4. Visualize your success in losing weight
5. Think about what motivates you
6. Uncover any emotional obstacles that may hold you back
7. Forgive yourself
8. Reward yourself for every achievement

Now go through the list and see if there are any topics that you might need to add or remove. Ensure that you remove only the topics that you find will be of very little interest to your readers and that it does not contribute much to the chapter.

Next, arrange all of the topics in the most logical order. In the example above, I felt that all of the topics were relevant to the chapter and I thought that potential readers will find this chapter very interesting. I then reorganized all eight topics and came up with the following:

How to Motivate Yourself to Lose Weight
1. Think about what motivates you
2. Choose a realistic goal
3. Create a diet plan that fits with your lifestyle
4. Visualize your success in losing weight
5. Set your priorities for losing weight
6. Uncover any emotional obstacles that may hold you back
7. Reward yourself for every achievement
8. Forgive yourself

The topics in the list above follow logically from one another. The whole chapter is about motivating yourself to lose weight so each topic is like an 8-step plan to get yourself motivated. It started from thinking about what motivates you all the way to rewarding yourself for your achievements and forgiving yourself if you stray from your diet plan.

Remember, when writing your book the chapters can be ordered in several different ways. Chapters could be arranged from simple to complex, or from theoretical to practical. They could be ordered by date, geographical location, by importance, or by comparison. Additionally, chapters could be ordered alphabetically or numerically. They could even be arranged by steps. No matter how you arranged chapters, you need to ensure that it makes life as easy as possible for the reader.

Arranging chapters in the best order is also beneficial to you as an author. This is because you will find it easy to write your book as one topic will flow naturally on to the next.

Convert Your List into Questions You can Answer

At this stage you should now have a complete outline for all the chapters in your book. This helps you to see all the topics your book will cover at a glance.

You could start writing your book at this point, but to make things even easier you can change the topics in your list to questions you can answer. It is a lot easier to write a response to a question than a plain title. For each chapter outline you created, go through your list of topics and turn each one into a question which the reader would like the answer to. If you cannot come up with a question, use the following – Who, What, Where, When, Why, and How.

For the example chapter above, 'How to Motivate Yourself to Lose Weight', I came up with the following questions:

How to Motivate Yourself to Lose Weight

1. What motivates you?
2. How do you choose a realistic goal?
3. How do you create a diet plan that fits with your lifestyle?
4. How do you visualize your success in losing weight?
5. How do you set priorities for losing weight?
6. What emotional obstacles are holding you back?
7. How do you reward yourself for every achievement?
8. Why do you need to forgive yourself?

After you have turned all the topics in your chapter outline into questions go through each of them and write below each one short phrases to sum up the answer. Be specific as possible. Here are the answers to each of the questions in the list above.

1. What motivates you?

Being optimistic about what is possible

Being realistic about setbacks that might occur

Making a public commitment

Using a good role model with a story that you can relate to

2. How do you choose a realistic goal?

Use the SMART method of setting goals

Set a specific goal

Make your goal measurable

Be accountable

Make sure your goal is realistic

Have a timeframe

3. How do you create a diet plan that fits with your lifestyle?

Determine your desired eating schedule

Determine how much time you will devote to food preparation

Get support

Devote time to exercise

Calculate calories

Design your daily meals and snacks

4. How do you visualize your success in losing weight?

Visualize your ideal body

Use visualization to reduce stress

Use visualization to work through your emotional issues

Use visualization to eliminate your junk food cravings

5. How do you set priorities for losing weight?

Start with the right frame of mind

Focus on sustainability rather than instant gratification

Focus on scientific research for losing weight

Focus on your appearance rather than numbers on a scale

Do more activities rather than exercise

Ensure that you are losing weight for yourself and not for someone else

Don't get obsessive about losing weight

6. What emotional obstacles are holding you back?

Bad habits

Eating for comfort

Embarrassed about going to the gym

Fear of fat

Procrastination

Depression

7. How do you reward yourself for every achievement?

Get a manicure/pedicure

Visit the pool

Buy a new outfit

Go bike riding

Socialize with friends and family

8. Why do you need to forgive yourself?

Helps to release negative judgements of yourself

Helps you to enter a world of love and positivity

You will eat healthier foods

You will talk to yourself with greater compassion

Negative feelings will lead you to turn to food for comfort or self-punishment

Chapter 6: Write Your E-book

If you have completed the whole process of outlining, then you are now ready to start writing your book. For now you are going to produce your first draft. Later you will then modify your book so that it will be read to be published. There are a couple of different ways you can write your book. Choose whichever method you feel comfortable with.

Writing Method #1: Free Writing

Free writing is a very useful technique often used by writers to boost their creativity. This method involves writing continuously for a set period of time, usually five to fifteen minutes, without worrying about spelling or grammar. It is a very effective tool which can help you to overcome writers' block.

This method may not be for everyone but free writing can be a very powerful tool for helping you to get your thoughts down on paper. Free writing not only helps you to generate ideas, but it is also known to relieve stress.

What happens is that you are actually unloading your thoughts onto paper. At the same time, those same thoughts that were flying around in your mind are being 'let go' which frees up space in your brain.

Writing Method #2: Voice Recording

Using a voice recorder to write your nonfiction book is a very effective tool to have. It is much easier to record your sudden bursts of ideas than to sit in front of a blank screen hoping that inspiration strikes. It is also beneficial when you find yourself nowhere near a keyboard or when you don't have access to a notebook and pen. Many authors use this method and it has helped them to complete the first draft of their manuscripts in a matter of days.

You don't need to purchase any expensive voice recorders or voice recognition software. A simple tape recorder will work just as well. There are also free voice recording apps that you can download on your mobile phone. Sometimes inspiration strikes at the most awkward moments and it is for this reason that a voice recorder will come in handy.

Just hit the record button and you will produce a massive output of words that you can type out later and edit.

What if You Have to do More Research?

When writing your book you may realize that you may need to do a little more research for certain chapters. It is highly recommended that you do your research after you have written your first draft. This will save you a lot of time and effort when writing your book.

If something comes up that you need to do a little more research on while writing your first draft, simply write a note reminding you to do more research on a particular topic or you can write in capital letters and brackets: (DO MORE RESEARCH ON THIS TOPIC).

Additional Writing Tips

There are several points that you should be aware of and even implement while writing the first draft of your book. This is the way a book is formatted so that it is easy for your audience to read it. Some of these tips you can use right away and some you can use when you start editing your first draft. We will cover editing your book in the following chapter. But for now, consider the following writing tips on how you should format your book.

1. Write your book in short simple sentences and paragraphs. These days people have the speed and convenience of simply downloading an e-book on their mobile device and start reading instantly. Because people are reading books more on screen than on a printed page, people find it more difficult because their eyes are focusing on a bright screen with a white background. If you decide to publish your manuscript as an e-book, and you want to make your book easy to read, you need to write short sentences and paragraphs to make your book as readable as possible. A short paragraph can consist of two or three sentences and a short sentence should only be one or two lines long.

2. Be sure to include plenty of white space in your book. Leave spaces in between your paragraphs and also leave extra spaces between sections. If you

have divided your book into chapters then I recommend starting each new chapter at the top of a new page.

3. Nobody wants to strain their eyes trying to read tiny fonts. Be sure to use a font that is big enough for people to read without straining their eyes. A size 12 font is perfectly adequate for the size of the text in your book. You should also use regular fonts such as Times New Roman, Arial, or Calibri to make your book more readable.

4. You can make your point clearer by using a lot of lists and bullet points. This is a great way to present related items of information.

5. If you publish an e-book, include active hyperlinks to other relevant websites within your book. Some of the hyperlinks can also be affiliate links to related products. If a person clicks on your affiliate link and buys the product, then you will get the commission. This can be extra profits you make in addition to your e-book income. Your hyperlinks

should lead the reader to websites that provide useful information and resources in addition to affiliate offers.

6. Avoid over-using graphics and images in your book. Depending on the platform you choose to publish your book, adding graphics may become a headache for the writer and an irritation to your readers. If you publish in e-book format, adding too many graphics will cause the file size of your book to increase and this may lead to long download times for the person who attempts to download your book. If a customer has a problem downloading your e-book, they may cancel their purchase and you will lose a prospective customer and potential sales. If you publish in print format, your images may appear blurry or pixelated because the resolution of your image was less than the required amount which is 300dpi (dots per inch).

7. If you do decide to use graphics, then make sure that they correspond with the relevant information. Your graphic could be an image, a table, a chart or

a diagram. These graphics can be used to explain a concept more clearly so that your readers will understand. You can also use free screen grab software to capture the screen of various web pages that you want to include in your book.

Once you have completed writing the first draft you can then move on to the next chapter which is about editing your book and getting it ready for publication.

Chapter 7: Edit Your Book

By this time you should have completed the first draft of your book. Congratulations! You deserve to give yourself a little treat.

But you still have a lot of work to do before you are able to publish your book. What you need to do now is go through your book and make the necessary changes so that it is in a suitable format for people to read.

Why is Editing Your Book so Important?

Nobody wants to read a poorly edited book filled with unclear images and poorly written text. This could have a negative impact on your sales and you could lose your readers. There are several other reasons why editing your book is so important.

1. The book you publish reflects you and your business, which means that it is essential that your book is free from spelling and grammatical mistakes.

2. It is very important to edit your book because you want to ensure that your book is the best it can possibly be.

3. A book that is not properly edited lacks professionalism.

4. You also need to ensure that your book is direct and easy to understand by your readers.

5. Failing to edit your book will make it difficult for you to make money.

6. A poorly written book could damage your reputation.

7. And finally, you need to edit your book to ensure that it is formatted correctly for publishing.

One thing you should know is that your book does not have to be perfect. You don't have to have a PhD in English to edit your book. I know that just the thought of editing may seem like a long and daunting task, but I am going to show you a very effective way how you can edit your book to ensure that it is up to a saleable standard. The entire process takes only four steps:

Step 1: Revise and edit your book on the computer. When you have completed the first draft or your book, go through it from beginning to end and correct any spelling and grammatical mistakes. If you are using Microsoft Word, use the spell checker to check the spelling and grammar. Click on the **Review** tab, and in the **Proofing** category click on **Spelling & Grammar**. However, do not rely on the spell checker only to revise your book. It is always better to revise and edit your work manually because sometimes the computer does not always pick up on words that are spelled incorrectly. It also tends to make the wrong suggestions as to how to correct grammar. So make sure that you do all the revising and editing yourself. When you are finished you will find that you have made a second draft of your book.

Step 2: Print a hard copy of the second draft of your book. Once again, from beginning to end, read through the entire second draft and write your notes in the margins. Note down all the changes you need to make to your book. Once you are satisfied, go back on your computer and make the necessary changes to your book. This will be the third draft of your book.

Step 3: Print a new hard copy of your book. This is the final step in the editing process. Read through your entire book aloud. Start from the beginning and don't stop until you reach the end. While you are reading, ensure that your sentences flow smoothly and that they make sense. Cut out and rewrite any words or phrases that cause you to stumble over the text. Make notes while you are reading so that you know what you need to do to improve the wording in your book. When you are finished, go back on your computer and make the necessary changes. Now you have completely finished editing your book.

Include Copyright Information

When writing your nonfiction book, don't forget to include the copyright information at the beginning and include a section about the author at the end. It is optional if you choose to write a short paragraph about the author. You can also include the URL of your website, your email address, and links to all of your social media networks so that your readers can connect with you.

You can find free copyright information by doing a Google search on the web. Some websites will even allow you to copy and paste the copyright info into your book.

The copyright page is usually located on the second side of the first page of your book. The first page contains the title of your book. The following is an example of what your copyright page should look like:

Copyright © 2015 by Christine John
All rights reserved.

No part of this book may be reproduced in any form or by any written, electronic or mechanical means including information storage and retrieval systems, without permission in writing from the author. The only exception is by a reviewer, who may quote short excerpts in a review.

Although every precaution has been taken to verify the accuracy of the information contained herein, the author assumes no responsibility for any errors or omissions. No liability is assumed for damages that may result from the use of information contained within.

Christine John
Visit my website at www.christinejohnbooks.com
Email: christinejohnbooks@gmail.com

Once you have completed the process of editing your book, you will be ready to move on to the next stage, which is designing your book cover.

Chapter 8: How to Design an Attention-Grabbing Book Cover

At this stage you should have completed the final draft of your book and it should be ready to be published. However, before you can publish your book you need to design an attention-grabbing book cover. There are two ways that you can go about designing a cover for your book. One way is to hire a professional book cover designer. The other way is to design the cover yourself. We will look at both methods.

Method 1: Hire a Professional Book Cover Designer

If you feel you do not have the skills or the time to design your own book cover, then your other alternative is to hire a professional designer. You can be sure that your book will have an attention-grabbing cover that will help readers to find your book. But a book cover designer can be very expensive. Prices range from $100 to $1000.

However, you can get a professional book cover made by visiting a website called Fiverr (www.Fiverr.com) where you can pay for a gig, i.e., hire a book cover designer for

$5.00. Once you pay for your gig, simply explain how you would like your book cover designed. You can upload a sample book cover image that you liked and you can explain to the designer what you want your book cover to look like. Specify the colour and style of your fonts, the colour of the front and back covers and the spine. Don't forget to mention the number of pages contained in your book so that the designer can make the correct measurements for the spine. Also you can upload the image you want included on your book cover. The designer may take up to seven days to complete the job. The best thing about Fiverr is that if you do not like the design of your book cover you can ask the designer to modify it for free until you are satisfied.

Method 2: The DIY (Design It Yourself) Book Cover
Most first time authors do not have a big budget to hire a professional designer to design a book cover for them. So they tend to design the book cover themselves. I personally have designed most of my book covers such as *How to Start and Run an Online Business*. It is not that difficult to design a book cover. Just follow the steps below and you will have an attention-grabbing book cover in no time.

Step 1: Consider Images and Fonts

Your book cover should tell your readers what your book is about. Think about what sort of image you want to use on your book cover and the type of font for the title, subtitle (if there is one) and the name of the author.

Step 2: Research the Covers of Other Titles in Your Genre

If you are having trouble coming up with an eye-catching cover page for your book, try looking at other titles in the same genre as yours. Go to Amazon and look up books in your genre. Consider the theme of your book. Is it a book about computers, marketing, employment, or space? For nonfiction books you may notice that many of the books have photos, diagrams or cartoon images. The title is usually larger than the author's name. Make sure that the images you use communicate the right message to the reader.

Step 3: Obtain High Quality Images

Once you have decided on the image you want to use for your book cover, you need to ensure that you find a high quality image. Go to www.FreeDigitalPhotos.net for royalty free images that you can download at no cost. Be sure to read their terms and conditions before you use the images from that website. If you download the image for free then you must acknowledge the author of the image, but if you purchase the image then you do not have to include any acknowledgements at all.

Step 4: Consider Different Formats

If you are simply publishing an e-book, the only thing you need to worry about is the front cover. But if you intend to publish in print format, then you will have to consider designing the spine and back cover of your book. Are you going to use an image for the front cover only or will the image wrap around the whole cover? You also need to keep in mind that the image resolution for print covers is much higher than the standard screen resolution for computers. Depending on the size of your image, it can come out blurry if you start from a small size and then increase it. You also need to remember that people shopping online will first see your book cover as a small thumbnail image. The title of your book and the author name may be difficult to read, therefore it is important that you ensure that the image of your book stands out.

Don't be too worried about designing your book cover. Whichever publishing platform you choose, there will be instructions to guide you through the designing of your book cover.

Parting Thoughts

My intention for writing this book is to help and inspire first time authors to write their own nonfiction book. In this book we covered finding the perfect writing environment, becoming an effective nonfiction author, how to do research on your ideas, how to write and edit your book and how to create a book cover.

The steps discussed in this book can be applied immediately and I suggest that you get started now. Don't waste another minute. All you have to do is research the market, write a high quality book, edit your first draft until you are satisfied with it, and then design a book cover. If you follow these steps and complete your first book, then you will find that it gets easier to write other books.

If you found this book to be very helpful in your writing endeavours, check out my second book in this series called *How to Publish a Nonfiction Book for Free Using Kindle Direct Publishing, CreateSpace, and Smashwords.*
I wish you all the success in the completion of your first nonfiction book!

Thank You

I hope that you found this guide to writing your nonfiction book to be very helpful. I want to say thank you for purchasing this book and for reading it all the way to the end.

I would be honoured if you could please leave a review for this book *How to Write a Nonfiction Book that Sells* on Amazon.

If you feel that this book answered your questions as to how to write a nonfiction book, then please do not hesitate to share it with your friends, family members and colleagues.

If you have any further questions or comments about this book or on writing in general, please contact me at the following email address:

ChristineJohnBooks@gmail.com

About the Author

"Effective Writing Strategies that Help and Inspire New Authors to Write, Promote and Sell Their Books."

Writing a book should be a fun and rewarding experience. But it can be difficult for new authors to write a book because they don't know where to begin or how to make money from their writing. Each of my books shows you how easy it is to write a book, publish it, and promote it so that you make money from your book sales.

Christine writes her books for new and established nonfiction book authors. What makes her different from other authors is that she explains the whole process of writing, publishing, and marketing books in an easy to read straightforward manner. She delivers step by step instructions you can follow and implement immediately.

Christine loves to travel, watching action/adventure and chick flick movies, reading and writing fiction and nonfiction books. She also loves to help and inspire others to make their dreams a reality.

Connect with Christine

Facebook

https://www.facebook.com/ChristineJohnBooks

Twitter

https://twitter.com/CejohnBooks

LinkedIn

https://uk.linkedin.com/in/cejohn

Google Plus

google.com/+Christinejohnbooks77

YouTube

https://www.youtube.com/user/SpringMediaIntl

More Books by Christine John

You can find all of these books on your local Amazon website. All of these books are available in Kindle and Print format.

Nonfiction

WordPress for Beginners: The Easy Step by Step Guide to Creating a Website with WordPress

How to Start and Run an Online Business

How to Get the Job You Want

Fiction

Last Chance

The Runaway Bride

Short Stories for Teenagers

Poems About Life